THE FACTS ON ASTROLOGY

John Ankerberg & John Weldon

HARVEST HOUSE PUBLISHERS
Eugene, Oregon 97402

THE FACTS ON ASTROLOGY

Copyright © 1988 by Harvest House Publishers
Eugene, Oregon 97402

ISBN 0-89081-715-4

Printed in the United States of America.

SECTION I

Introduction to Astrology

Astrology is once again in the headlines. Not as in 1975 when 192 leading scientists, including 19 Nobel prize winners, publicly disavowed it.[1] This time astrology is in the headlines because of the influence it has achieved at the highest level of national government, the White House. The unforeseen result has been a literal flood of new public interest in astrology.

1. What is astrology?

Astrology is a belief system based on the assumption that the stars or planets (as interpreted and configured by the astrologers themselves) mysteriously influence the lives of men. Astrology teaches that this influence begins at birth and continues throughout a person's life. Thus the *Shorter Oxford English Dictionary* defines astrology as "the art of judging the occult influence of the stars upon human affairs."

The following are representative definitions of astrology that are given by astrologers themselves:

1) "Astrology is the study of the heavens...and the influence they exert upon the lives and affairs of humanity."[2]

2) "Astrology is the science of certain cryptic [hidden or mysterious] relations between the celestial [heavenly] bodies and terrestrial [earthly] life."[3]

3) "Astrology is the science of life's reactions to planetary vibrations."[4] ("Vibration" here is something mysterious that supposedly works like the moon's gravity influencing the ocean tides on earth.)

4) "Astrology is the system of interpreting *symbols* [heavenly bodies that are assigned names and influence by astrologers] correlated to human behavior and activities."[5]

There are many kinds of astrology: 1) *Ancient* astrology was practiced by the Babylonians. They taught that the planets were gods and as such the planets ruled and influenced life on earth (some occult groups using astrology today have similar beliefs); 2) Those holding to *material* astrology believe that "emanations" or "influences" from actual planets in our solar system rule or affect life on earth; 3) Those who believe in *symbolic* astrology teach that the stars and planets are only *symbols*. They go on to assume that there is a mysterious "magical correspondence" revealed by the symbols which influences life on earth.

There are many other kinds of astrology each with different assumptions. Nevertheless, here we have three kinds of astrology with three different sets of assumptions. The planets are either 1) gods, 2) impersonal heavenly objects, or 3) just symbols. Yet all three claim they are responsible for producing the same conclusion: Whatever the planets are, they influence life on earth. But as Bertrand Russell once observed, when two views both claim to be true but contradict each other, one or the other may be true, but they both can't be true at the same time. The same can be said about astrology. Logically, the different kinds of astrology can't all be true when they contradict each other. It remains to be seen if any one of them is true.

2. How does astrology supposedly work?

Astrology supposedly "works" by the planets or stars affecting our lives. The main tool astrologers use for interpreting this alleged influence on our lives is the astrological chart, called a *natal* [birth] *horoscope*. (Strictly, the term *horoscope* also involves the interpretation (delineations) of the chart, although the terms "chart" and "horoscope" are used interchangeably.) This chart calculates the exact position of the heavenly bodies at the moment of birth, usually from the baby's first breath. The baby's first breath is crucial with most astrologers because they accept a premise of magic called "correspondences" (that everything in the heavens is correlated; thus, events in heaven parallel events on earth). Thus, for them the child's first breath permanently "stamps" him with the corresponding heavenly stamp or pattern existing in the sky at that moment. It is this unique, impressed pattern stamped upon the child that astrologers believe determines one's character and ultimately his destiny.

For some astrologers the "permanent stamp" is the influence sent out by the heavenly bodies absorbed by each of us as we draw our first breath at birth. Some astrologers say these heavenly bodies send out influences which forever determine up to 80% of our potential personality and destiny.[6]

For still other astrologers, the heavenly stamp is not claimed to correspond to the actual planets. It is assumed to correspond to mysterious influences that astrologers interpret by their symbols. Nevertheless, one way or the other, for our entire lives, astrologers claim that the heavenly planets continue to influence in predictable ways based upon our original pattern at birth.

In addition to the birth horoscope, astrologers use secondary charts. For example, a *mundane* chart will examine the fortune of cities, states or countries. An *electional* chart is drawn up to decide the best time to undertake some activity. The *horary* chart is composed to answer questions on any given topic. Why are all these secondary charts important? Because the heavens are in motion. Astrologers say that since the planets change their positions in the heavens, it is necessary to have new charts made to determine their current influence on us. These secondary charts (called *progressed horoscopes*) give us more specific information to relate to our birth chart. This additional information supposedly reveals to us how we are likely to act and choose.

Thus a chart may be drawn at any particular moment of time by astrologers to determine particular heavenly influences that may affect us. The information received supposedly helps the client to make decisions in such areas of life as love and relationships, family, financial matters, occupation, etc.

Whether or not the stars or their magic symbolism really influence us, one fact should be clear. Once we accept the premises of astrology, it does not matter. Astrology does indeed exert a powerful influence but it is because of the person's belief in astrology itself, not the influence of the stars. For example, the power we grant to the astrologer to accurately interpret the alleged heavenly pattern or influence acting upon us is a dramatic yielding of the direction of our lives. For many people, no major decision will ever be made without first consulting an astrologer. Also because astrology claims to reveal the future, it will always have power, for the desire of many to know the future cannot be underestimated.

Astrologers claim to be able to predict both the heavenly influences on our life at the present moment and for the future. These two powerful categories of motivation (decisions about the present and information concerning the future) that lead people to astrology are also discussed in the Scriptures. God gives guidance for responsible decision-making concerning the present moment. He also promises to help us in the future (Ps. 46:1; 48:14; 73:24; Mt. 6:25-34; 28:20; Phil. 4:1-20; Heb. 13:5). If a person has a choice between going to an omniscient, infallible counselor or a fallible human being, would it be logical to choose the latter? If one can go to a loving and trustworthy source, why go to an unproven and questionable counselor? God has a proven record; astrology does not, as we will soon see.

3. What are the basic terms and concepts necessary to an understanding of astrology?

Why is astrology so often confusing to the average person? It is because of its complexity and the many unfamiliar words which astrologers use.[7] The following definitions and concepts are basic if one is to understand astrology.

The *Zodiac* is an imaginary "belt" of sky containing the 12 astrological signs or constellations around which the ancients built imaginary human and animal figures. (The Zodiac and the constellations are both imaginary geometric configurations.)

The *signs* are the "signs of the Zodiac" also known as "Sun-signs." Everyone is born under one of these 12 signs or constellations (Pisces the fish, Leo the lion, Gemini the twins, Taurus the bull, etc.).

The *houses* are the 12 sections of the Zodiac which together symbolize every aspect of life. The planets move through the houses; thus, when a planet falls into the sphere of the given house, it comes under its respective influence. The astrologer plots all of these factors and more on a chart. This chart is called a *horoscope*.

The *horoscope* is a "map" of the heavens at the moment of the birth of a person or any specific time thereafter. On this chart, an astrologer plots the positions of the "planets," "signs," and "houses" for a given moment. The chart is then interpreted by numerous complex rules, many of which vary greatly from one astrologer to another.

A mental picture might be helpful in understanding the basic ideas of astrology that we just defined. But we should first understand that the "world" of astrology is based upon an ancient view of the universe, not a modern scientific one. The ancients constructed their view of the universe based entirely on how things *appeared*. Thus looking up at the sky at night, it appeared as if the stars and planets were moved along the inner surface of a great hollow globe, a celestial sphere. The sun, moon, and planets appeared to revolve around the earth, etc.

Now imagine a huge glass ball with a thin white belt encircling it. According to astrology, the *glass ball* is the *celestial sphere*. The *white belt* encircling the glass ball is the *Zodiac*. Divide the *white belt* into 12 sections. Each of these sections is given a name. The name is of a symbolic animal or man representing the imaginary *constellations* known as Aries the ram, Virgo the bull, Leo the lion, Gemini the twins, etc. These symbols of animals and men are called the "*signs of the Zodiac*" or the "Sun-signs." This is what is meant when people say, "my sign is 'Libra,' 'Pisces,' 'Aries,' 'Gemini,' " etc.

If one could look inside this glass ball and see a tiny green marble at its center, this would be symbolic of the *earth*. And if one divides all the space inside the glass ball into 12 sections, these sections would represent what the astrologers call "houses." These sections would start at a point in the middle of the glass ball (the green marble—the earth) and extend out to the Zodiac or the encircling white belt. However, these 12 house sections are spaced differently from the 12 Zodiac sections along the white belt. Inside the glass ball the astrologers place the Sun, Moon and eight other planets. As these planets move, they move through the 12 sections on the white belt, the Zodiac, and also enter and pass through the 12 different sections of space called the houses.

In addition to all of this, astrologers believe that each planet "rules" or especially influences different signs of the Zodiac. For example, Mercury rules or influences Gemini and Virgo, whereas Venus is said to rule or especially influence Taurus and Libra.

One more important term used by astrologers must be defined. Astrologers use the word "aspect." Aspect refers to the angles between the planets as seen or plotted on a horoscope chart. Certain angles are interpreted as good and some angles are bad. For example, two planets angled at 90 degrees to each other (called a "square") supposedly exert a bad influence. However, two planets angled at 120 degrees to each other (called a "trine") supposedly exert a very good influence. But it is more complicated than this. Astrologers also must take into consideration whether the planets are "good" planets or "bad" planets. The words "good" and "bad" as referring to angles or planets has been defined by the astrologers. But why are these angles and planets logically defined as good or bad? Even the astrologers don't know; they simply accept them and point to their astrological tradition that has been passed on for centuries. To be fair, some astrologers would say these definitions are the result of thousands of years of observing human experience. But no one has accurately recorded 4,000 years of human experience. And if they had, why are there so many conflicting astrological theories?

To show how subjective astrological interpretation is, ask any astrologer how he knows the different houses represent different things. For example, how does he know that the first house represents personality, the second house money, the third house communication, the eighth house death, the tenth house occupation, etc.? Astrologers have designated many different aspects of life to each of the different houses. The question is, "On what basis do they logically do this?" Again astrologers claim this information comes from 4,000 years of human observation. But again, such observation has never occurred and if it had, then astrologers should agree with each other on their interpretation. Astrologers may also say these meanings were derived from numerology—from the meanings allegedly inherent in numbers which were then related to astrological theory. But if these meanings were derived from numerology, we still cannot explain a logical reason why such a system should be true or valid. In addition, to show the extent of disagreement, astrologers do not even divide the houses in the same manner. This means that a given house for one astrologer may be a different house for another, and therefore entirely different influences would be suggested.[7a]

Also by determining when a planet crosses or "transits" a specific point on the horoscope chart, the astrologer feels he can advise a client as to "favorable," "unfavorable," or cautious times concerning a given activity. Thus just as there are good and evil planets and angles, there are good and bad days for undertaking certain activities. This was why Hitler planned his war strategy by the stars and why even some American presidents have sought the advice of the stars as to the planning of their activities.

4. How influential is astrology today?

Astrologers West and Toonder believe that astrology now "enjoys a popularity unmatched since the decline of Rome."[8] Science writer and engineer Lawrence E. Jerome makes the astonishing claim that at least one *billion* people around the globe "believe in and follow astrology to some extent."[9] Bernard Gittelson is a New Age human behavior researcher and former public relations consultant representing the West German government, the European Common Market, the U.S. Department of Commerce, and other major clients. He calculated that the circulation of newspapers and magazines carrying astrological columns in the U.S., Europe, Japan, and South America totaled over 700 million or three-fourths of a billion.[10]

In the United States, the interest in astrology has fluctuated but remained high. For example, in 1969 *Newsweek* estimated there were 10 million committed believers in astrology and many more dabblers. In 1975 a Gallup poll indicated over 32 million Americans believed "that the stars influence people's lives" and in addition that many of them consulted their daily or weekly horoscopes.[11] Not only that, but estimates of the number of astrologers ranged as high as 10,000 full-time and 175,000 part-time.[12] Ten years later, a Gallup poll in 1984 revealed that among teenagers (aged 13-18), 55% believed in astrology. This figure was up from 40% in 1978. A 1988 Gallup poll indicated 10% of evangelicals believe in astrology.[13]

Today in the West, astrology is the subject of over 100 magazines, and the topic of millions of books in print. Since 1960 the annual production of new titles has doubled every ten years.[14]

Astrologers claim "there is no area of human experience to which astrology cannot be applied."[15] Many occult practices (numerology and Tarot cards) have logical connections to astrology; many world religions and religious cults (Hinduism and Theosophy) have their own brands of astrology; and astrologers have even attempted to integrate many of the sciences (medicine and psychology[16]).

Proof for the astrologer's claim that there is no area of human experience to which astrology cannot be applied can be seen by checking your local bookstore. For example, the smallest sampling of astrology titles indicates its potential for wide applications: *Your Dog's Astrological Horoscope; Your Baby's First Horoscope; Astro-power at the Racetrack; The Teenager's Horoscope Book; Cat Horoscope Book; Pluto: Planet of Magic and Power; Chinese Astrology; Cooking With Astrology; Diet and Health Horoscope; Earthquake Prediction; Medical Astrology; The Astrologer's Guide to Counseling; Horoscope of Murder; Find Your Mate Through Astrology; Astrology and Biochemistry; Astrological Themes For Meditation; Sex Signs; An Introduction to Political Astrology; Astro Numerology; Stock Market Predictions; Homosexuality in the Horoscope; The Astrology of I Ching; Sex and the Outer Planets; From Humanistic to Transpersonal Astrology; Financial Astrology; Astrology and the Edgar Cayce Readings; Aztec Astrology; Astrology and Psychology; Woman's Astrology; Esoteric Astrology; Hindu Astrology; Astrology and Past Lives; Astrology: Key to Holistic Health; Astrology, Alchemy and the Tarot; Asteroid Goddesses; Astrology of Theosophy; Astrology in the Bible; Horoscope of Canada; A Guide to Cabalistic Astrology*, etc.

Research scientist Geoffrey Dean estimates there are as many astrologers in the western world as there are psychologists.[17] And over 80% of all U.S. newspapers now carry horoscope columns.

Astrology today also can boast an impressive list of "who's who" believers. Today a few notables include: Prince

Andrew and Fergie, Princess Diana, Hollywood stars Robert
Wagner, Phyllis Diller, Jill St. John, Angie Dickinson,
Lauren Bacall, Goldie Hawn, Olivia Hussey, Rona Barrett,
Olivia Newton-John, Debbie Reynolds, Joan Collins, Liza
Minnelli, Arlene Francis, Jane and Peter Fonda and many
others.[18]

Today astrology is offered for credit on some high school
and college campuses.[19] Some corporations seek astrological advice for major decisions and over all, astrology is
estimated to be anywhere from a $200 million to a one-
billion-dollar-a-year industry.[20] In fact, a cable news net-
work (CNN) report cited astrologers who claim that "at
least 300 of the Fortune 500 [companies] use astrologers in
one way or another."[21]

5. Why is astrology so popular?

Astrology is popular because it claims to provide important information that people want to know. Astrology claims
to provide people with information that will: 1) protect
them, 2) bring them success, 3) guide them, 4) predict their
future and 5) help them understand themselves.

Astrology offers people the belief that they can "control"
their own destinies, and it also provides them a ready-made
justification for failure or sin. Astrology offers the false hope
that through the "knowledge" of the stars, one can manipu-
late people or events for his own welfare or selfish desires.
Astrology specializes in answering almost all the questions
people ask concerning the future. In fact, it claims to offer
power over life and death, love, sex and relationships, money
and finances, personal health and happiness, etc.

Above all, astrology sells hope—and today people need
hope desperately! In every age of social breakdown, the
masses of people have turned to the occult and superstition
for solace and counsel. Today is no exception.

In conclusion, astrology is popular because it claims to
offer people hope through the knowledge of the manipula-
tion of the influences of the planets and stars. With this
secret knowledge, people believe they have greater control
over themselves as well as present and future circumstances.

6. Can newspaper horoscopes be dangerous?

The first horoscope column appeared in the *London Sun-
day Express* in 1930.[22] In the next 50 years, horoscopes were
slowly incorporated into 80% of American newspapers; that
is, into 1,250 out of 1,500. Most professional astrologers

complain that these columns are vastly oversimplified at best and "utter nonsense" at worst.[23] This is true even though professional astrologers often write these columns (such as Sydney Omar and Carroll Righter). It is also true that professional astrological organizations give seminars on how to write the columns.[24]

Most newspaper editors reject astrology and seem to believe that horoscopes are simply an amusing pastime for their readers.[25] But are the conclusions of these editors true? Could it be true that modern newspapers are being socially irresponsible for the following reasons?

1) Newspaper horoscopes seem to bear at least some responsibility for the modern revival of interest in astrology.[26] The law of averages tells us that a certain number of these very general "predictions" found in America's newspapers will come true, or will be interpreted as coming true by the people who read them. One can only wonder how many people have turned to astrology after months or years of reading their horoscopes. Even the occult encyclopedia *Man, Myth and Magic* stated: "The daily forecast and the feature articles in magazines have persuaded countless thousands that the 'stars' may conceivably influence human destinies...."[27]

2) Astrology has been shown to be both false and dangerous.[28] Obviously to encourage something that is untrue, irrational and superstitious is not in society's best interest.

3) Astrology is a proven occult art. By virtue of its many connections to numerous other forms of occultism (such as witchcraft and spiritism), astrology is a potential introduction to a much wider practice of occult activity. Newspapers would not think of carrying columns giving advice on witchcraft or spiritism but they do not hesitate to offer astrological "counsel." In conclusion, astrology leads to occult involvement. Occult involvement has been proven dangerous[29] and for all Christians is condemned by God (Deut. 18:9-12; Is. 47:13; 1 Cor. 10:20).

For these reasons and more, it is therefore irresponsible for newspapers to continue carrying astrological columns.

SECTION II

Astrology and the Occult

7. Is astrology related to the occult?

We may define the occult, in general, as the attempt to secure supernatural power or knowledge. The Christian believes that this occult knowledge and power come from spirit beings that the Bible calls demons.[30] Astrology is related to the occult in four major ways. First, astrology itself is defined by Webster's Dictionary as an occult art. As such it employs occult practices such as divination. Divination may be defined as "the art of obtaining secret or illegitimate knowledge of the future by methods unsanctioned by and at variance with the holiness of God" and which involves contact with evil spirits.[31] Secondly, astrology appears to work best when the astrologer himself is psychically sensitive, what most astrologers would term "intuitive." Thirdly, prolonged use of astrology often leads to the development of psychic abilities.[32] Fourthly, due to its history and very nature, astrology often becomes the introductory course to a wider spectrum of occult practices. All of this points to the fact that the very practice of astrology is a foundational occult art and that the practitioners (astrologers) open themselves up to becoming involved in other occult practices.

Nevertheless modern astrology wishes to be seen as scientific. As a result, we are told that as a system of belief, it has nothing whatever to do with the occult and that the astrologer himself need not be psychic at all, although he may be "intuitive." An example of this is leading astrologer Carroll Righter who "feels strongly that astrology should not be considered [part of] the occult."[33] Because of his practice as an astrologer, "he regards himself as a scientist..."[34] Another influential astrologer, Charles E. O. Carter, claims "astrology does not involve any form of psychism..."[35], thus showing his aversion to the occult. Practicing astrologer Colette Michaan states "astrology is magical only in the sense that insight is magical."[36]

These quotes remind us of the pronouncements of the parapsychologists who similarly claim that when they study psychics and mediums they are only studying "natural" and "normal" human powers—nothing occult, supernatural or spiritistic. But such claims are false whether made by parapsychologists or astrologers. Author John Weldon has shown that parapsychologists unwittingly have opened themselves to demonic powers under the guise of latent human abilities.[37] If astrologers wish to truly be seen as scientific, it is natural to expect they would not admit to the occult nature of their craft. But instead we could expect them, like parapsychologists, to define their craft in modern scientific and psychological terms. But have astrologers misstated the case? Can it be documented that astrology by nature is part of the occult? Finally, is there a connection between the astrologer and psychic abilities?

From its inception, astrology has been tied to the world of paganism, magic, spiritism, and the occult and this remains true today. For example, in examining two dozen "channeled" books (revelations given by a spirit possessing someone's body), astrology was accepted or endorsed in almost all of them.

Proof that the spirits (demons) are clearly interested in promoting astrology can be seen in the following two examples.[37a]

First, one of the spirits who communicated through mystic and occultist Alice Bailey (founder of Lucius Trust) telepathically transmitted many books to her, including *Esoteric Astrology*.[38] A second example is Edgar Cayce, who was a powerful medium. Throughout most of his life the spirits speaking through him endorsed the practice of astrology. The 14,000 readings Cayce gave in trance are considered the largest single body of psychic information in the world. Over 2,500 of them dealt with what were termed "life readings" and "almost all [of them] refer to past incarnations and specific astrological or planetary influences bearing on the present."[39] When asked if it was right and proper to study astrology, the spirits that spoke through Cayce said "very very very much so."[40]

The spirits are not the only occult connection to astrology. In terms of occult realities, astrology and the occult go hand in hand because they are fundamentally inseparable. There are historic ties between the rise of astrology on the one hand and the corresponding turning to the occult on the other. It is also true that where there has been the rise of the occult there has also been a corresponding turning to astrology. For example, Helena P. Blavatsky was a potent medium and virulent antagonist of Christianity. She founded one of the most influential occultic movements in modern Western culture, known as the Theosophical Society. Astrologers West and Toonder have pointed out the influence of Theosophy on the modern American revival of astrology: "It is to Ms. Blavatsky and the Theosophical Movement she founded that astrology owes its revival.... Theosophy, in one blow... inspired a renewed and serious inquiry into astrology, first in England, then not long after in Germany, France and America."[41] (Actually it was Theosophy and two other occult societies—Rudolph Steiner's Anthroposophy, and modern Rosicrucianism—which are responsible for America's renewed passion for astrology in the twentieth century.)

Next, it can be noted that most occultists use astrology and that many astrologers practice other occult arts. For example, astrologer Daniel Logan admits he is involved with mediums and spirits;[42] astrologer Marcus Allen has a spirit guide and studies yoga, Zen, Tibetan Buddhism and Western magical traditions, etc.[43]

And it is not surprising that both astrologers and occultists admit that astrology is a pillar of occultism. In his *A Manual of Occultism*, "Sepharial" states: "The astrologic art is held to be the key to all the occult sciences."[44]

In her book *My Life in Astrology*, famous witch Sybil Leek states, "Astrology is my science, witchcraft is my religion..."[45] She calls the horoscope "a magical document."[46] She also claims astrology is "a vital tool" for using magic and observes its connection to numerology, phrenology, palmistry and witchcraft.[47]

In her *An ABC of Witchcraft Past and Present*, witch Doreen Valiente observes: "Astrology...is another of the fundamentals of magic. It is studied by witch and magician alike."[48] Thus, when "a witch wants to select an herb to use for a magical purpose, she has to use one whose astrological rulership [remember the planets rule the signs] is correct for the work in hand...the Moon rules psychic things, and an herb of the Moon, mudwort...is used to make an infusion or tea which many believe is an aid to clairvoyance."[49]

Some astrologers admit that astrology is an occult practice. For example, the field of "humanistic" and "transpersonal" astrology combines astrology with Eastern philosophy, the occult and Jungian psychology. Theosophist Dane Rudhyar is the leader in this field. In his book *The Practice of Astrology*, he states that "the astrologer has authority as one who deals understandingly and effectively with...the occult." He then says "astrology is threshold [by this he means occult] knowledge."[50]

Henry Weingarten is a leading astrologer, director of the National Astrological Society in New York, and author of the multi-volume series titled *The Study of Astrology*. In his studies he has concluded that astrology is related to palmistry, numerology and Tarot cards. He also admits "almost all occultists use astrological timing [that is, the best time as set by astrology] in their work."[51] Then he quickly adds, "Most astrologers are not occultists." When Weingarten claims that most astrologers are not occultists, he allows his philosophical "slip" to show.

Not only do many astrologers and virtually all occultists admit that astrology is part of the occult, but so do objective scholars who have studied the subject. Richard Cavendish was the main editor of the 24-volume encyclopedia entitled *Man, Myth and Magic* and also *Encyclopedia of the Unexplained: Magic, Occultism and Parapsychology*. He was educated at Oxford University and considered a leading authority on the history of magic and occultism. In his book *The Black Arts* he observes: "Astrology is essentially a magical art ... astrological considerations have always been extremely important in magic ... some magical textbooks classify the 'spirits' ... in terms of their planetary affiliations."[52]

In his definitive study of sixteenth and seventeenth century English occultism, *Religion and the Decline of Magic*, Oxford-educated historian Keith Thomas documents the strong intellectual and practical links between magic, divination, astrology and witchcraft.[53] He shows that much of occultism is actually undergirded by an astrological worldview. He also documents that some medieval astrologers claimed to get their knowledge of astrology from the spirit world. For example, he mentions a spirit named "Bifrons" that made men "wonderfully cunning" in the subject of astrology.[54]

In *Astrology Disproved*, science writer and engineer Lawrence Jerome concludes that of all the occult "sciences," astrology appears most scientific but is really "nothing more than a magical system for controlling others."[55] He states, "Astrology, then, has played a major role in all the magical 'sciences': alchemy, black magic, the conjuring of spirits, necromancy, and even in the simpler magical practices such as the use of talismans."[56]

Trial lawyer and philosopher Dr. John Warwick Montgomery asserts that astrology is "found virtually everywhere occultism is to be found."[57]

Other scholars believe that among certain people, astrology provides a logical connection for a conversion to the occult practice of Satanism. In "Magical Therapy: An Anthropological Investigation of Contemporary Satanism" sociologist Edward J. Moody explains there is a certain psychological need for control and power in many whom (because of their disposition) he classifies as "pre-Satanists." He shows how this need naturally finds its expression first in astrology. It then logically progresses into Satanism which provides a "more powerful means of control" of one's fate. Everyone should take notice of Moody's frightening conclusion that "those who eventually become Satanists usually have begun with astrology..."[58]

In summary, if astrologers say their craft has no associations to the occult they are either uninformed or they are lying.

8. Do some astrologers claim to use psychic abilities?

The attempt to maintain a scientific image and to avoid the occult image of their practice requires most modern astrologers to stress the "objective" nature of interpreting their chart or horoscope. For example, astrologers enjoy informing the public that astrological information is so objective that they can look up chart information in the "standard" manuals of astrological interpretation (for example, what Pluto in the seventh house means). This sounds good but hardly makes astrological interpretation objective.

Astrology is anything *but* looking at facts to make authoritative interpretations. There is obviously a great deal of subjective and "intuitive" assessment by each astrologer in explaining a horoscope for a person. Many astrologers, who care little about maintaining a scientific image, admit astrological practice often utilizes or requires a *psychic* sensitivity. (The *Oxford American Dictionary* (1982) defines psychic as that which is "concerned with processes that seem to be outside physical or natural laws, having or involving extrasensory perception or occult powers.") This shouldn't surprise anyone. After all, astrology is defined even by Webster's Dictionary as an occult art. It is also a fact of research in this area, that continued occultic practice and use eventually tend to develop psychic abilities in a person.[59]

Right at this point, some astrologers play word games. They say they are merely developing and using the "intuitive" powers which lie dormant in everyone. Astrologers have adopted the modern myth promoted by parapsychologists (those who scientifically study occult phenomena) that everyone has psychic potential. As a result, they may claim they are not engaging in anything supernatural or "psychic." Yet, when pressed, the astrologers we contacted admitted that "intuitive" and "psychic" were one and the same word for them. These astrologers prefer the word "intuitive" because for many people the term "psychic" has too many negative occult connotations, while the word "intuitive" is far more neutral, positive, and universal to people's ears. Thus, just as the old negative terms of mediumism and spiritism have often been replaced with the modern New Age term "channeling," the old occultic term psychic has for many people now been replaced by the new word "intuitive." For example, psychic researcher Bernard Gittleson talked to "dozens of astrologers" and observed, "though many adepts [experts] feel *psychic* to some degree, most spoke of their *intuitive* senses without necessarily calling themselves *psychic*."[60] (emphasis added)

The question that must be answered is, "Are *all* astrologers psychic?" Truthfully, even though all astrologers practice an occult art, this does not mean every astrologer is necessarily psychic. It is common knowledge that there are standard "cookbook" methods for interpretation of astrological charts that anyone can buy. But some astrologers do openly classify themselves as "psychic astrologers." And one astrologer even went so far as to tell us that all *genuine* astrologers were psychic by definition. Yet some astrologers never seem to develop psychically, and others may require years to become psychic. However, we believe the vast majority eventually do. One former astrologer believes that because of their abilities, all true astrologers are sooner or later subject to spiritistic inspiration, whether or not they are personally conscious of being psychic.[61]

For example, when interpreting the chart, astrologers may feel mild to strong "impressions"; they may notice they are "led" to certain data, or find themselves saying something unexpectedly. Information derived in this way turns out to be highly important to the client and may involve information about the client that the astrologer could not possibly have known. Yet, the fact is that many spiritists are guided by their spirit guides in a similar manner. Thus Robert Leichtman, M.D., states of his spirit guides: "What they did was to give me a whole bunch of ideas. And of course I thought, well, my mind has suddenly become brilliant. It was already great before, but now it is absolutely brilliant. I was getting all kinds of ideas from time to time and of course, the spooks [spirits] said they were giving them to me, [but at first I didn't believe it.]"[62]

It is hardly surprising that many astrologers would seek to develop themselves psychically, for astrologic philosophy encourages this. For example, "the Piscean is [told he is] highly intuitive, and can develop psychic and mediumistic abilities."[63] Astrology teaches that when "Pisces is on the ascendant and Aquarius rules the twelfth house," this can indicate a high degree of psychic potential.[64] Any number of different combinations of astrological interpretations may encourage an astrologer or his client in the direction of psychic development. Famed astrologer Sidney Omar admits that "with Uranus in the fifth house" he had to find outlets for his "need for expression" and these were "magic, the occult...palmistry, numerology, psychic phenomena."[65] Some astrologers associate the planets Uranus, Neptune and Pluto with development of psychic potential.[66] In addition, the public is told that if the Moon, Mercury, or Venus are in the twelfth house; if the Moon is in Sagittarius or Aquarius; if Mars and Jupiter are in Cancer; or if there is a Jupiter-Saturn conjunction in Taurus, all of these can indicate mystical, psychic, or intuitive potential.[67] And these are only some of the total possible combinations that may indicate this.

That astrology often does depend upon psychic ability is recognized both by occult authorities and astrologers themselves. In *The Occult: A History*, Colin Wilson observes that astrology, like palmistry "...depends upon an almost mediumistic faculty."[68] The occult encyclopedia *Man, Myth and Magic* refers to astrologers who excel at horoscope interpretation as having "highly developed intuitive powers."[69] Humanist astrologer Michael Shallis believes astrological knowledge comes through intuition.[70] Astrologer Julien Armistead says, "I don't think you can read an astrological chart if you're not intuitive." Astrologer Charles Jaynes claims he does "not think a non-intuitive astrology works very well at all, because it *can't*."[71] (emphasis added) But astrologers Jane Gosselin and Julien Armistead candidly admit they do use psychic abilities to interpret the chart.[72] Dr. Ralph Metzger, a famous explorer of consciousness through drugs and the occult, observes in his *Maps of Consciousness* how the astrologers' psychic processes may work: "...astrological horoscope casting is in one way a framework for intuitive perception. I know of one clairvoyant astrologer who simply looks at the actual horoscope diagram and then begins to 'see' the inner life, the thought forms, and emotional patterns of her client, almost as if she were gazing into a crystal ball."[73]

It must be pointed out that some astrologers clarify the source of their intuition and psychic ability. For example, astrologer Marcus Allen has written *Astrology For the New Age: An Intuitive Approach*. In this book he thanks "my spirit guide for his insight and clarity and presence."[74]

So what we have seen here is that despite the many claims to being scientific, astrologers often admit their practice involves psychic abilities, and some even admit to having spirit guides. Of course, not all astrologers would admit to having a spirit guide. But isn't it interesting that those who do not admit to having spirit guides have the same powers as those who do?

SECTION III

Astrology vs. Christian Belief

9. What do astrologers think about God?

If an astrologer claims to be a Christian, attends church and reads his Bible, and claims that his practice of astrology is compatible with his Christian belief, would you believe him? Is there any conflict between Christian belief and astrology? What would you say to Christian laymen who think there is nothing wrong with checking their horoscope each day? In reading and asking practicing astrologers to put their beliefs about God in brief form, most would say something like this: For them, the idea of pantheism (all is God; God is all) defines their belief in God. Others say they are not opposed to belief in God, in whatever shape or form a person wishes to believe. What is clear is that almost 100% of the astrologers do not arrive at their views of God from reading the facts of the Bible.

The astrologer who has formed his view of God from data other than the Bible has a different God than the biblical God. He is more in agreement with the common view that teaches "the Fatherhood of God and the Brotherhood of man." Whether you are an atheist, Hindu, Buddhist, or Moslem or hold to almost any view of God at all does not bother them. As long as anyone allows astrology, they do not care what they believe about God. This is the view of God they accept. However, astrologers are opposed to believing in a God who defines certain actions and deeds as being wrong—as sinful—and obviously astrologers are opposed to someone who believes in a God who condemns the practice of astrology. And finally, like the majority of people in the world, they do not accept the views of our Lord Jesus Christ who said, "no man can come to God but by Me" (Jn. 14:6). That is, they don't believe that Jesus is the Savior of the world who forgives their sins by His death on the cross and our faith in Him (Jn. 3:16; 5:24; 6:47).

Many astrologers define God in such a way that their belief easily blends within an occult view of the world. For example, for the majority, God is seen existing as a divine power and in some sense all life and all Nature are seen as divine.[75] This is why witch-astrologer Sybil Leek writes, "God is in everyone," including Nature, and she sees no conflict in using astrology as a major means of practicing witchcraft.[76] Another astrologer states that astrology is an "affirmation of the Divine order in the universe" which enables one "to align oneself with the energies of Nature" and realize that the "planets are our sources of energy . . ."[77] Another astrologer states that true astrologers are spiritually oriented "healers" who know that they are "only the channel through which the Power [inherent in creation] flows" and "but a channel through whom the energies can flow."[78] Unfortunately, when astrologers look to nature and the creation for divine wisdom or empowerment, "nature" often becomes a "smoke screen" (a disguised worldview) that allows spirits or demons to provide occult powers to the astrologers. This power includes revelation, the intuition to give startling true information about a person from the horoscope. Again, when astrologers give this kind of information, it is very similar to what happens when spiritists give information to people through the power of their spirit guides.

In addition, astrology really rejects God for His creation. Both the idea of a personal creator God and man's responsibility before Him are abandoned. The result is that men are no longer responsible to God, but only to themselves and to some impersonal force.

In conclusion, astrology rejects the biblical teaching on God and adopts occultic views which give to God's creation the glory due to God alone. As Dr. Robert Morey states, "it is idolatry to ascribe to the stars that which belongs *only* to the God who created them."[79]

10. What does astrology believe about Jesus Christ?

It is clear that astrology is willing to accept every view of who Jesus Christ is except the view that Jesus Himself taught and what the Bible teaches. The second thing to be noticed is that astrologers typically adopt an occultic view of Christ (for example, that Jesus the man was reincarnated on the earth and that "Christ" is our "higher self"). Note two leading astrologers' views of Jesus Christ. Ronald Davison is "England's foremost living astrologer" and has been editor of *The Astrologers Quarterly* since 1959. He states, "the story of the most perfect Being whoever incarnated on earth tells of the ultimate sacrifice on the cross . . . for the purpose of paying off any remaining debts [karma] of his own to the past. . . ."[80] Notice here that this prestigious astrologer believes Jesus was just another spirit who was reincarnated on the earth. Davison sees Christ's death on the cross as necessary for paying the price of His own "sins" (karma).

Marcus Allen is another example of a professional astrologer who teaches an occult view of Christ. He believes

Christ is now everyone's higher occult self. Thus he states, "Christ had all seven ancient planets...all conjunct in Pisces...so he was the supreme, the ultimate Pisces...and so he initiated the Age of Pisces which is now coming to an end with the dawning of the Age of Aquarius, which is initiated by the second coming of the Christ Life within *all* of us.... In the Age of Aquarius, everyone is the Avatar, everyone is tuned into their higher self..."[81]

What Allen is saying is that Jesus Christ was the supreme illustration of the Piscean temperament or personality. However, what Allen believes is that since the Age of Pisces is now passing and the Age of Aquarius is started, the Second Coming of Christ is the beginning of a period of higher "consciousness" for all men. In other words, this professional astrologer concludes that Christ Himself, through His "return," is equal to the emerging occult consciousness of all humanity. This view is in conflict with what the Bible teaches. The Scriptures teach that Jesus Christ is fully man and fully God in one person, the only begotten Son of God and Savior of the world, who will return someday physically and visibly to the earth (Mt. 24:1-35; Jn. 1:1; 3:16; 10:30; Acts 1:11).

11. What does astrology believe is man's basic problem and its solution?

Most astrologers believe the problem of man is that he is out of harmony with the divine forces and energies of the universe. He must become united with this harmony. And therefore, for many astrologers, salvation is not forgiveness from sin (most astrologers do not believe in sin in a biblical sense) but rather an enlightenment as to the underlying divine pattern they say governs the universe. "Salvation" is becoming aware of the powerful effect of these celestial patterns. Many astrologers believe that through a "higher consciousness," which is supposedly a joining with the divine evolutionary "impulse," that this will eventually bring a mystical Oneness with what they call "God" or ultimate reality. Astrologer Dane Rudhyar has written of the one who accepts astrology, "he learns to identify his consciousness and will with the 'celestial' patterns and rhythms." He goes on to say that the person "becomes one with the principles of universal order, which many call 'God.' "[82]

On the other hand, the Bible teaches that we are rebellious creatures who willfully ignore God and commit endless sins. Salvation is a free gift that delivers us from God's wrath against our sin and is based on our believing Christ died for us and receiving this gift by faith (Jn. 3:16; Rom. 5:1-10; Eph. 1:7; 2:8-9; 1 Pet. 2:24).

In addition, most astrologers also believe in reincarnation (one survey revealed about 75% of astrologers believe this[83]). Reincarnation teaches that over many lifetimes men will die and come back to life and eventually evolve back into the state of their original oneness with God. Astrology is seen as a guide and a tool to enlighten men during each life to avoid adding more karma, thus quickening the day when they will attain their true divine nature. However, the Bible teaches we do not have an endless number of lifetimes to perfect ourselves; we have only one lifetime in which to decide either to accept God's forgiveness or face His righteous judgment after death (Heb. 9:27; Rev. 20:10-15).

12. What does the Bible say about astrology?

The Bible teaches that astrology is not only a futile (worthless) activity, but an activity so bad that its very presence indicates God's judgment has already occurred (Acts 7:42-43). As both a philosophy and practice, astrology rejects the truth concerning the living God and instead leads people to dead objects, the stars and planets. As it mocks idols, the Bible mocks astrologers and their practice (Is. 47:13).

However, this has not prevented most astrologers from claiming the Bible favorably supports astrology. Jeff Mayo, founder of the Mayo School of Astrology, states, "the Bible is full of astrological references."[84] Joseph Goodavage, author of *Astrology: The Space Age Science* and *Write Your Own Horoscope*, claims that "the Bible is full of" the philosophy of astrology.[85]

Astrologers "justify" such statements in the same way many cults quote the Bible as evidence for their own false and unbiblical teachings. They twist the Scriptures until they teach something contrary to the Bible.[86] Any Scripture which refutes such false teachings is simply ignored, misinterpreted or deleted. It can be proven that every single biblical text that astrologers quote to prove the Bible supports astrology has been either misinterpreted or misapplied.[87] Just as oil and water do not mix, the Bible and astrology are utterly irreconcilable. Even non-Christians admit there is a "permanent ideological wedge between the two beliefs."[88]

Christianity has historically been opposed to astrology for three biblical reasons. First, the Bible explicitly rejects astrology by name as a futile (worthless) practice. Proof of this is Isaiah 47:13-14 where God states, "All the counsel you have received has only worn you out! Let your astrologers come forward, those star gazers who make predictions month by month, let them save you from what is coming upon you. Surely they are like stubble; the fire will burn them up. They cannot even save themselves...." Here we can see that first, God is condemning the counsel of the Babylonian astrologers. Second, God says their predictions based on the stars will not save them from what is coming: divine judgment. Third, God says the counsel of the astrologers is not only worthless to others but it cannot even save the astrologers themselves. (See also Deut. 4:19; 17:1-5; 18:9-11; 2 Kgs. 17:16; 23:5; Jer. 8:2; 19:13; Ezek. 8:16; Amos 5:26-27.)

The second biblical reason Christianity has historically opposed astrology is because God forbids occult practices. Astrology is basically divination. Divination is defined by *Webster's New Collegiate Dictionary* (1961) as "the act or practice of foreseeing or foretelling future events or discovering hidden knowledge." In *Webster's New World Dictionary* (1962) it is defined as "the art or practice of trying to foretell the future or the unknown by occult means." Because it is an occult art, God condemns divination as evil and as an abomination to Him and says it leads to contact with evil spirits called demons (Deut. 18:9-13; 1 Cor. 10:20).

Finally, the Bible rejects astrology because it leads people to the horrible transference of their allegiance from the infinite God of the universe to the things which He has made. It is a bit like ascribing all the credit, honor and glory to the masterpieces of art themselves, completely forgetting the great artist who made them. No astrologer, dead or living, would have ascribed the works of Rembrandt or Picasso to the paintings themselves, yet they routinely do this with God. And yet God is infinitely more worthy of honor than men, a God who "made heaven and earth" and in whose hands is their very life's breath (Gen. 1:1; Dan. 5:22-23).

13. Does the book of Daniel support the practice of astrology?

Astrologers often say the book of Daniel is proof of God's acceptance of astrology. First, they say this is true because God made Daniel the head of the astrologers and magicians in Babylon (Dan. 2:48). Second, if he was the head of all the Babylonian "wise" men, he must certainly have been proficient in astrology, for Babylon was widely known for its astrological practices. But this is not true. Why? The first reason this is not true is that the biblical account of Daniel explicitly attributes all of Daniel's success to God alone, not to his alleged practice of astrology or to the stars (Dan. 1:17; 2:27-28; 4:17-18). Second, Daniel was a godly man who, according to his own testimony, abhorred the idolatrous and evil practices of Babylon (Dan. 1:8; 4:27). Third, it is unthinkable that God would permit Daniel to engage in the very practices for which the nation itself was now in judgment (astrology, idolatry, etc.) Fourth, proof that Daniel did not embrace astrology is seen in the fact that he pointed out the constant failures of the Babylonian astrologers compared with the true knowledge given by God. Far from endorsing astrology, Daniel rejected it and pointed men to the one true God. Thus the entire book of Daniel reveals the uselessness of astrology. The astrologers had a failure rate of 100% when compared with the one true God (Dan. 2:27-28; 4:7; 5:7-9,12-13,17).

God was the One who was sovereign, but the Babylonian kings had turned to the stars for advice and ignored the true God. For example, in Daniel 5 he pronounces judgment upon the Babylonian ruler Belshazzar by stating "but you his son, O Belshazzar, have not humbled yourself, though you knew all this. Instead, you have set yourself up against the Lord of heaven . . . You praised the gods . . . which cannot see or hear or understand. But you did not honor the God who holds in His hand your life and all your ways" (Dan. 5:22-23). When divine glory and power are given to the "gods" of the heavens and not to the God who made the heavens, God says, they have "exchanged the truth of God for a lie and worshiped and served created things rather than the creator—who is forever praised" (Rom. 1:25). In fact this is the very reason why God's judgment comes. It comes because men ignore Him and suppress the truth in unrighteousness; thus "the wrath of God is being revealed from heaven against all the godlessness and wickedness of men who suppress the truth by their wickedness, since what may be known about God is plain to them, because God has made it plain to them. For since the creation of the world God's invisible qualities—His eternal power and divine nature—have been clearly seen, being understood from what has been made, so that men are without excuse. For even though they knew God, they neither glorified Him as God nor gave thanks to Him, but their thinking became futile and their foolish hearts were darkened. Although they claimed to be wise, they became fools and exchanged the glory of the immortal God" for false idols (Rom. 1:18-22).

In other words, astrology is condemned in the Bible because its very practice indicates a form of idolatry already under divine judgment: "But God turned away [from them] and gave them over to the worship of the heavenly bodies" (Acts. 7:42-43).

In conclusion, astrology is rejected in the Bible because it 1) is futile and worthless, 2) constitutes involvement with occult powers and 3) is a form of idolatry (exchanging the heavens for God). Thus it 1) has no power to save men from their sins, 2) opens men to demonic deception and 3) robs God of the glory that is due Him.

14. Is there such a thing as Christian astrology?

We have just seen that the Bible completely rejects astrology. Any comprehensive study of Christian history presents a strong testimony against astrology, despite astrologers' claims to the contrary.[89] The only brief period in which some in the church ever "embraced" astrology was a period in which the Bible itself was largely rejected and the church was full of evil practices, immorality and paganism.[90]

In spite of all this, there are three categories of those who are astrologers and yet who claim the Christian faith: 1) those who claim to be Christians simply because they live in a "Christian" country or were raised in a nominal Christian environment, yet they have no association with any church or doctrinal faith whatsoever; 2) those who actively practice a pseudo form of Christianity and attend a church that is not biblical; and 3) those who say they accept biblical authority yet still practice astrology. However, one cannot *logically* hold to both Christianity and astrology. We shall now briefly examine these three categories.

Category 1—Many astrologers *claim* to be Christian, yet in reality they are hostile to Christianity! Dr. Robert Morey has observed, "even though the majority of astrologers claim to be Christian, they are generally hostile to the teachings of historic and biblical Christianity."[91] These people who claim to be Christian would probably admit themselves they have a preference for occultism (however they define it) and that they are not *biblically* Christian.

Category 2—Then there are those with moderate-to-strong church affiliation who say they are Christians but nevertheless reject the Bible as the final authority in matters of astrology. Their faith is usually in God in a general sense. They do not admit to knowing God personally and show little interest in being born again (Jn. 3:3-8). Since these people practice astrology and reject God's instruction on this topic, the following verses may apply to them. "They claim to know God, but by their actions they deny Him" (Tit. 1:6). Or, "If we claim to have fellowship with Him yet walk in the darkness, we lie and do not live by the truth" (1 Jn. 1:6). Or, "The man who says, 'I know Him,' but does not do what He [God] commands is a liar, and the truth is not in him. But if anyone obeys His word, God's love is truly made complete in him. This is how we know we are in Him: whoever claims to live in Him must walk as Jesus did (1 Jn. 2:4-6).

It is sad to say that many Americans believe that psychic Jeane Dixon is a good Christian. Yet in her book *Yesterday, Today and Forever* she states she was guided by the Holy Spirit in integrating Christianity and astrology.[92] She claims:

> "Some of my friends consider this a strange practice for a Roman Catholic. As I understand it, however, the Catholic church and many other religious bodies as well has never condemned the study of astrology.... I have never experienced any conflict between my faith and the guidance I receive from my church on the one hand and the knowledge I find in the stars on the other ... actually, much of what I know about astrology I learned from a Jesuit priest, who was one of the best-informed scholars I have ever met."[93]

She relates that it was through a series of visions that she was led to adopt astrology. She says that from these visions, she discovered:

> "the answer which could pull together the facts of Scripture and the data of astrology ... now I understand why, in my vision, each apostle was associated with a different Zodiac sign; for each was being revealed to me as to the archetype of that sign. Each [apostle] embodied all the mental and emotional characteristics of his own segment of the Zodiac ... that simple yet profound truth was the message I received both through my meditations and in subsequent visions during the following weeks."[94]

She concludes:

> "...astrology fits into God's plan for mankind by helping us understand both our talents and our shortcomings. Being better informed about ourselves, appreciating our strengths and aware of our weaknesses, we will be much better equipped to turn everything we are [over] to the service of the Lord."[95]

(To understand why Jeane Dixon is wrong concerning her views on astrology, see the comments below in Category 3.) In continuing to discuss those who categorize themselves as Christian astrologers we must reluctantly admit that in spite of all the Bible says against astrology there have been a few true Christians who have embraced astrological views.

Category 3—Dr. John Warwick Montgomery refers to Lutheran scientists Tycho Brahe and Johann Kepler as Christian men who "were convinced that astrology was not incompatible with divine revelation."[96] A man wrote to us claiming to be a "Christian professional astrologer" and wanted us to know that he finds "no clear and specific injunction against astrology and the Bible." In presenting his defense to us he said, "True, astrologers are called to task for...misuse of their skills—as are prophets, priests and kings—but are not called to deny or shun the practice of those skills." He went on to say:

> "Indeed, *worship* of 'the starry host' as it is translated in the NIV is forbidden to the believer; as is *worship* of money or 'the king'; but a respectful *observance* and *stewardship* of economic and political forces is not only permitted, but required."

> "Scripturally, only if astrology is assumed to be divination can we find it placed off limits for God's people; and most astrological counseling is not divinatory in nature. Moreover, while the Scriptural warnings about divination read as though they were absolute, we find in comparing Scripture with Scripture that the Covenant People were divinely provided with an oracle, the Urim and Thummin, which was to be used *only at the hands of the member of the Covenant Community.*"

> "The practical inference is that it is wrong for believers to enlist the skills of *unbelievers* when they wish to discern the will of God—

with which I heartily agree; for to do so places one in spiritual jeopardy." (emphasis added; in other words he believes Christians *are* permitted to consult Christian astrologers—such as this individual!)

"It is my conclusion, therefore, that astrology—like any other human art or science, such as nuclear physics or psychotherapy, can be useful when carried on in submission to the Lordship of Jesus Christ; but is spiritually and psychologically dangerous when practiced in the spirit of the world, the flesh, or the devil."[97]

This is essentially the same argument "Christian parapsychologists" use. (Christian parapsychologists scientifically study the occult and among other things, apply it to the church.) Like Christian astrologers they claim that the Old Testament condemnation of mediumistic and spiritistic practices (Deut. 18:9-12) was only intended for those who misused these practices, but was not meant to condemn those who use such practices "ethically," "wisely," with good motives, and for God's glory.[98] However, Christian astrologers and parapsychologists ignore the fact that God specifically called these practices in and of themselves evil. God Himself failed to make any fine distinctions on such practices. Proof that there is no such fine line made by God as to Christian astrology or Christian spiritism is seen in the fact that God makes such fine distinctions when they are important. If Christian astrology or Christian spiritism *were* important to spiritual growth, we should expect that God would have made such a distinction. After all, God has done so in many other cases. For example, sex is glorified within marriage but condemned outside of marriage or among persons of the same sex. God also says that certain foods and drink are permissible in one situation, but not in another (Rom. 1:26-27; 14:20; 1 Cor. 6:18). The basic argument of the Christian astrologer is that astrology can be beneficial as long as one is not *worshiping* the stars (which would be idolatry) or engaging in *divination* ("the act or practice of trying to foretell the future by occult means"), but this is a false conclusion. It is a conclusion based largely upon pragmatism (if it works, it's okay). They say astrology "works" and is "helpful or useful," therefore, it should not be condemned. But if this reasoning is true, then why not try and strip all other forms of the occult of their divination and idolatry and, as Christians, simply glean their "wisdom" and practical uses?

But the arguments of Christian astrologers never address these six important issues: 1) Can astrology really be separated from its occult connections? 2) Are the basic premises and principles of astrology scientifically accurate? 3) Can it be said that astrology is in any sense concerned with moral principles? 4) Does Scripture really justify the practice of astrology for any purpose? 5) What are the unforeseen risks or consequences of practicing astrology (see Question 23)? and 6) Why would God forbid astrology if it were really so helpful? After all, would God totally condemn any practice if it were even slightly good?

SECTION IV

Critical Evaluation of Astrology

15. Is the scientific evidence for astrology valid?

In the last question we answered the assertions of those who claim there is such a thing as Christian astrology. We will now examine the evidence from science that astrologers claim validates their practice. For this booklet, we attempted to secure the best scientific evidence available on behalf of the claims of astrology. For example, we contacted the largest and most scientifically oriented astrological society, The American Federation of Astrologers in Tempe, Arizona. This organization offers almost 1,000 books for sale, over 600 tapes and claims to be "the nerve center of astrology in America today..." The AFA also claims that for 50 years it has been the leader in "astrological education and research."[99]

But the literature they recommended as giving the best evidence for astrology was both disappointing and questionable.[99a] The most important research they cited was the Gauquelin research which we will discuss below. It must first be said that much of astrology is simply not scientifically testable because of the very nature of astrology. For example, it claims to be a practice based upon mystical influences and private, subjective interpretations of individual astrologers reading the horoscope. That is why (at these points) astrology can never be *scientifically* proven or disproven. Its phenomena lie outside the boundaries of science ("intuition," mystical planetary influences, symbolic correspondences, etc.). Nevertheless, both astrologers and scientific investigators of astrology agree there are definite astrological principles which merit scientific testing.[100] But if these prove false, and if the practical results of astrology are *better* explained by nonastrological data, then our only conclusion is that there is simply no evidence for the truth of astrology.

The overall evidence astrologers set forth to prove their case may be divided into three basic categories: 1) the general arguments, 2) statistical studies, and 3) practical results (the third issue is the most important and the one most often cited. For our critical analysis see Question 22).

First, the common arguments as put forth by most astrologers are examined by Kelly et al., and summarized by research scientist Geoffrey Dean. Dean noted that Kelly, et al., said that none of these arguments cite *valid* reasons for belief in astrology. (Remarks in parentheses are theirs.)

1) Astrology has great antiquity and durability. (so has murder)
2) Astrology is found in many cultures. (so is a flat earth)
3) Many great scholars have believed in it. (many others have not)
4) Astrology is based on observation. (its complexity defies observation)
5) Extraterrestrial influences exist. (none are relevant to astrology)
6) Astrology has been proved by research. (not true)
7) Non-astrologers are not qualified to judge. (so who judges murder)
8) Astrology is not science but art/philosophy. (not a reason for belief)
9) Astrology works. (the evidence suggests otherwise)[101]

The second area of evidence astrologers set forth to prove the validity of astrology comes from certain statistical studies. We are unable to cite all major studies here, but we can briefly cite the negative results of four major studies. We may also state that *every* other study we are aware of encounters the same or similar problems as these.

Please note that the following studies have all been claimed as evidence or proof of astrology. Yet nothing could be further from the truth.

1) The *Mayo-White-Eysenck Study* attempted to determine if astrology could predict in advance whether the personality of adults would be introverted or extroverted. It was done with 2,324 adults who had their extroversion/introversion scores tabulated on the Eysenck Personality Inventory (EPI). These scores were then correlated with astrological predictions. Their conclusion: *Marginal* (read favorable) results were obtained that could not be accounted for by chance alone. Five additional studies revealed: three did not support these findings, two did. Finally, it was discovered later that the positive results could be adequately explained in a number of different ways, *without* recourse to astrological theories. Eysenck himself in later research (confirmed by other researchers) came to believe that "the entire astrological effect [of the original study] was due to the subject's expectation and familiarity with the characteristics associated with their Zodiac sign."[102] In brief, this study cannot be used as evidence for validating astrology.

2) The research involving the *Gauquelin "Mars" Effect* became a scientific study to test if the birth dates of 2,088 sports champions were statistically significant according to "astrological" predictions. What researchers concluded was that a statistically significant number of sports champions were born when Mars was situated between the eastern horizon and the celestial meridian. This means that a correlation of 21.65% (of those sports champions born at the above time) existed against an expected chance correlation of 17.17% (the number of sports champions normally expected to be born).

The "Mars" Effect has never been absolutely confirmed in 20 years of subsequent studies. The most that can be concluded to date is "the success of replication [could these same statistics be confirmed?] is a matter of some debate."[103]

Significantly, even though Gauquelin's research is often noted by astrologers as confirmation of astrology, Gauquelin himself has done perhaps more definitive research than anyone else to disprove it. His work involved seeking out possible *cosmological*—not *astrological*—influences. (Gauquelin's so-called "neo-astrology" is not related to astrology proper and is still subject to debate.) Yet he has examined the claims of astrology and tested them in great detail. In one study he used 15,560 subjects to test the alleged influence of the Zodiac in relationship to professional success. Gauquelin concluded: "the results were entirely negative."[104] When astrologers objected that "professional success" was "far too crude a criterion to reveal the astral subtlety of Zodiacal influences," Gauquelin established further elaborate testing to satisfy their complaints and substantiate his conclusions. (Note: Astrologers *do* claim the heavens influence the likelihood of professional success.) Nevertheless the astrologers said that Gauquelin should have tested not professional success but *personality*, and they claimed if he did so then he would have found a real influence. It is important to notice here that when data seemed to confirm astrology, the astrologers accepted the criteria of professional success for the sports champions, but when the same criteria disproved astrology, they rejected it. In spite of this, Gauquelin obliged the astrologers and tested personality traits with Zodiacal predictions. In his test, 52,188 personality traits were systematically collected from 2,000 subjects. What did he find?—only that astrological predictions received "a fatal blow."[105]

Read almost any book by a scientifically minded contemporary astrologer and most likely you will find him citing

Gauquelin's works as evidence for astrology. Yet just the opposite is true; Gauquelin himself never claimed to prove astrology. For example, Gauquelin has authored *The Scientific Basis of Astrology: Myth or Reality* (1973) and *Dreams and Illusions of Astrology* (1979). Listen to what Gauquelin himself forcefully stated about the scientific validity of astrology: "Every attempt, whether of astrologers or scientists to produce evidence of the validity of astrological laws has been in vain. It is now quite certain that the signs in the sky which presided over our births have *no power whatever* to decide our fates, to affect our hereditary characteristics, or play any part however humble in the totality of affects, random and otherwise, which form the fabric of our lives and mold our impulses to action. *Confronted with science*, modern and traditional astrology are seen to be imaginary doctrines."[106] (emphasis added)

3) The massive *Guardian-Smithers Study* tested 2.3 million people comparing occupations and Sun-signs. Although a *mild* correlation was noted, Smithers himself remained unconvinced. He concluded that most of the data "can be explained in other ways" (for example, seasonal factors, social habits, belief in astrology, etc.). Later, a further reevaluation of Smithers' research claimed design flaws. It was also noted that effects could be explained by additional nonastrological factors.[107]

4) *The National Enquirer* test examined 240 people and correlated their astrological sign and personality. They claimed to show that 91% of the people tested had their personality determined by their Zodiac sign. However, subsequent testing failed to substantiate the *Enquirer's* claims.[108]

In conclusion, the scientific evidence cited in favor of astrology turns out to be no evidence at all. Just the opposite is true—in fact, science disproves astrology.

16. What is the scientific evidence against astrology?

The scientific evidence against astrology is extremely conclusive. Yet the response of astrologers to this fact is simply to ignore it. Astrology has always lived in its own private world, impervious to all assaults. As one critic remarked, "The situation is not helped by the typical astrologer's attitude toward factual evidence so well described by Levy (1982), [a man] who runs Australia's largest computerized chart calculation service: 'I often get the feeling, after talking to astrologers, that they live in a mental fantasy world, a kind of astrological universe where no explanations outside of astrological ones are permitted, and that if the events of the real world do not accord with astrological notions or predictions, then yet another astrological technique will have to be invented to explain it.' "[109]

Among astrologers there is a stubborn refusal to face the facts, and they often exhibit a fundamentally *irrational* approach. For example, note the comments of the chairman of the United Kingdom Astrological Association, who is critical of the astrologer's inclination for excuses. He is describing what an astrologer can do to "harmonize" astrological predictions with a person who does not match them. In this case below, he is describing a person who is very meek, but who astrology predicts should be aggressive:

> "If I found a very meek and unaggressive person with five planets in Aries, this does not cause me to doubt that Aries means aggression. I may be able to point to his Pisces Ascendant, or to his Sun conjunct Saturn, or to his ruler in the twelfth house; and, if none of these alibis are available, I can simply say that he has not yet fulfilled his Aries potential. Or, I can argue (as I have heard argued) that, if a person has an *excess* of planets in a particular sign, he will tend to suppress the characteristics of that sign, because he is scared that, if he reveals them, he will carry them to excess. But if on the next day I meet a very aggressive person who also has five planets in Aries, I will change my tune: I will say that he *had* to be like that because of his planets in Aries."[110]

Astrology is a modern myth that millions believe. Just as millions once believed the stars were gods, today millions believe the stars influence their character and destiny. Yet to date, dozens of tests have *failed* to prove astrology. The comprehensive nature of this scientific testing conclusively invalidates astrology. In the following questions, we will examine some of the tests for specific tenets of astrology.

17. What have the tests for Sun-sign validity proved? (For example, are you a Pisces, Aries or Leo?)

According to astrology a person's Sun-sign is said to have the greatest importance in determining his overall character.[111] One researcher's analysis of the content of astrological literature revealed 2,375 specific adjectives for the 12 Zodiacal Sun-signs. Each sign was described by about 200 adjectives (for example, "Leo" is strong, domineering, tough—a born leader; a "Taurus" is indecisive, timid, insecure—not a leader). In this test, 1,000 people were examined for 33 variables, including physical attractiveness, leadership ability, personality traits, social and religious belief, etc. The conclusion was that this test failed to prove any astrological prediction: "All of our results can be attributed to random chance."[112]

There was another test to find out if the planets influenced compatability in marriage. That is, was there any significant indication of numbers of couples who, because their signs showed they were "compatible," stayed married? Did those born under an "incompatible" sign get divorced? This study involved 2,978 couples who got married and 478 couples who got divorced in 1967 and 1968. This test proved that astrological signs did not significantly alter the outcome of either group. Those born under the "compatible" signs married and divorced as often as those born under the "incompatible" signs.[113]

Astrologers claim that scientists and politicians are favored by one Sun-sign or another. That is, there is supposed to be a connection between a person's Sun-sign and his chances of success in a given profession. John McGervy, in doing research on this topic, compared birth dates of 16,634 scientists and 6,475 politicians and found no correlation to substantiate the astrologers' claims. There can be no doubt the distribution of signs among these two professions was as random as for the general public.[114]

In conclusion, the scientific evidence today shows there is no validity to the astrologers' assertion that your Sun-sign influences your life.

18. What have the tests for horoscope validity proved?

At least seven independent studies have indicated that even with the best astrologers there is *little agreement as to the meaning* of a chart.[115] (emphasis added)

In addition, seven other studies revealed that people who have horoscopes interpreted for them cannot tell the difference between a right chart and a wrong chart. That is, they are just as likely to identify someone else's horoscope rather than their own as being the one that they think best describes them. In other words, the tests showed that people were just as happy with wrong charts (someone else's chart) as they were with right charts. Thus, researchers found that the interpretations "fit" people even when the interpretation was from the wrong chart. (These results could *not* be

explained away by astrologers blaming poor chart interpretation or by astrologers claiming the people lacked knowledge of themselves.[116])

In fact, many tests reveal that people cannot even tell
authentic charts from charts that have been deliberately
reversed. People rated reversed charts just as highly as
authentic charts. It is obvious that reversed charts are
diametrically the opposite of authentic charts. Therefore,
the conclusion people drew from these two horoscopes could
not have been more wrong.

In conclusion, these tests show that people tend to accept
any chart as valid for a variety of reasons (about 20)[117]
wholly unrelated to astrological theory (such as gullibility,
expectation, emotional need, etc.).[118]

And what's worse, researchers found that astrologers
who used charts were no better in their judgments than
those astrologers who did *not* use charts—who were just
guessing. In fact, the research showed that astrologers who
used charts made worse judgments.[119]

19. What have the tests for the influence of the Moon proved?

Space limitations require that we be brief. Nevertheless
over three dozen scientific studies (see footnote) have failed
to indicate *any* "causal relationship between lunar phenomena and human behavior."[120]

20. What have the tests for astrological predictions proved?

These tests have revealed that astrological predictions
have an extremely high failure rate. For example, one large
study examined over three *thousand* predictions by leading
astrologers and leading astrology publications from 1974 to
1979. This study revealed a 90% failure rate in astrological
predictions.[121]

The editor of *Free Inquiry*, Dr. Paul Kurtz, has written
that "there have been exhaustive tests of astrological claims
to see if they have any validity" and yet despite the fact that
astrologers claim to have a 4,000-year record of success and
that this record speaks for itself, "dozens of scientific tests of
astrological columns, charts and horoscopes clearly contradict this claim."[122]

We may state fairly and accurately that it has scientifically been proven that the heavens do not influence us in

the manner astrologers claim. To our knowledge, astrology has failed every test ever given.

Yet all of the scientific disproof of astrology still cannot explain how astrologers can sometimes provide true self-disclosures to their clients (information they have no way of knowing), or how in rare cases they are accurate in their predictions. As we shall see in Question 22, it "works" for reasons fully unrelated to astrology itself. Some of these reasons are natural ones and some of them are supernatural, but in no case are they astrological.

21. What do astrologers believe about astrology?

It appears that as a whole, many or most astrologers do not think very highly of their craft or even of other astrologers. First, even some astrologers admit that most other astrologers are frauds. John Townley, a respected U.S. astrologer with 20 years experience, admitted the following, "I would say that most of the accusers of astrology are probably correct. They think that astrologers are 100% charlatans, but I would bring it down to 90%. [They are] not necessarily...intentional charlatans.... [but] Maybe 50% of the people are deliberately selling hokum straight ahead."[123]

Second, many astrologers admit to the reality of contradictory and false theories within astrology. For example, Kathleen Russo and Carolyn Burmingham, president and vice president of the Federation of Scientific Astrologers admit that "Much of what has been proposed by astrologers in the past and today is without foundation and should be considered 'nonsense'..."[124]

Third, astrologers themselves admit many interpretations of horoscopes are unfounded and uncertain. For example, astrologer John Addey admits, "So far as the practical rules of horoscopy are concerned there are a host of uncertainties—[concerning] the Zodiac, the houses, aspects—all [of them now] present intractable problems..."[125] In addition, astrologer Dr. W. M. Davidson wrote that astrology was largely a failure and that "many [of its] interpretations are just a mass of generalities, haphazard guesses..."[126]

Fourth, concerning scientific testing, Charles Carter, editor of *Astrology Magazine* and recognized as "one of the world's outstanding and most knowledgeable astrologers," states, "Statistical research, such as early astrologers could not carry out for lack of sufficient data, has [now] cast considerable doubt on the validity of portions of the rather incoherent mass of tradition that till recent years represented astrological science."[127] S. Best, the editor of *Correlation*, the scholarly journal of research into astrology, has concluded: "We really have no alternative. Either we put our house in order or someone from the establishment will sooner or later take great delight in doing it for us, or, alternatively, taking it apart brick by brick."[128]

In conclusion, to date we have found the scientific evidence against astrology is conclusive, and that astrology itself, according to astrologers, is in a state of disarray and confusion. These findings prepare us to examine what astrologers claim is the key "proof" of astrology—that "it works." But we must ask, if it is not true, how can it work?

22. If astrology is false, how can it work?

Astrology works for reasons unrelated to astrology. Consider the dilemma of modern astrology. Every test given proves it is false. Astrology schools and theories contradict one another. Astrologers themselves are depressed over the state of astrology. The astrologer has no recourse but to claim that it *must* be true, since it works. Yet if we can show that it does not work for any reason related to astrology, then no astrologers can logically claim that it works because it is *true*. And if it is not true, then a massive campaign of consumer fraud is being foisted upon the public. If a man purchases a car that he is promised works on gasoline and yet it only works on nuclear power, he is up the proverbial creek.

Knowing *how* something works can be more important than knowing *that* it works. If astrology claims it works because of celestial birth patterns, and yet it only works because of reasons related to human psychology, or as we shall see, spiritistic deception, then the consumer has been deceived. He was promised objective knowledge of stellar influences to help him better live his life. In fact, what he got was a con that in the end opened him to the occult and other dangers. Astrology does not need to be true in order to work, but the reasons *why* it works make it potentially dangerous. If astrology is offering occultism to people in the disguise of celestial influences, it is both morally and spiritually dangerous. When astrologers offer "knowledge" of the future to people based on their unproven theories or under the guidance of spirits, people should be warned of the consequences.

Astrologers see the arguments against astrology as no arguments at all because astrology seems to work and who cares if we can't explain *why* it works.[129]

If people knew astrology was false, and that it only worked by self-deception or demonic spirits, and that it was also dangerous, can we believe they would continue to consult astrologers?

It has been shown that psychological factors can account for a great deal of astrology's success.[130] What about the supernatural spirits called demons? Are they related to the startling self-disclosures that are sometimes found in astrology? Psychic researcher Bernard Gittelson states:

> "One friend of mine was amazed that on the first visit, her astrologer was able to pinpoint major life events, that the astrologer could never have known about, to specific two-week periods that occurred twenty years before they met. In other words, don't be surprised by what your astrologer knows about you."[131]

Consider the following assessment of a former professional astrologer:

> "...as we look honestly at astrology, we begin to see that adherents of this system—without knowing it—are banging on the door through which communication is established with knowledgeable yet deceptive spirit beings. Eventually that door opens. And that opening produces an appalling development in the adherent's life. He or she matures in the craft in a most unthought-of manner: as a spirit medium. Without contact with spirit beings, there would be no astrological self-disclosures. Or if they did come, [without spirit contact] it [supernatural information] would be almost entirely from guess work; [and] they [supernatural self-disclosures] would be very rare."[132]

But if it is not possible to distinguish between astrological self-disclosures and those given through the spirit world in general, then, in light of all that we have seen, it is more logical to conclude that these amazing disclosures derive from spiritistic sources—not from the stars. In addition, when astrology is seen to be an occult practice, often using or developing psychic abilities, and when we find the same tragedies and deceptions as found in spiritism, then how can we believe the astrologers when they say that it is merely the stars which are influencing us?

23. Are there dangers for those who believe in or practice astrology?

Some things work extremely well but are nevertheless quite dangerous; for example, guns, dynamite and car bombs.

The dangers of astrology (and of all forms of divination) can be divided into six basic categories: 1) physical damage, 2) inducements to crime, 3) economic loss, 4) psychological damage, 5) spiritual damage and 6) moral damage.

1) *Physical damage*—For example, even some astrologers admit that because it is often quackery, "medical astrology is an area often fraught with many pitfalls."[133] Thus when an astrologer advices a client against his child's appendectomy and the child dies as a result, this is more than tragic.[134]

2) *Inducements to crime*—Dr. Kurt Koch observes that "astrology has been responsible for a number of suicides and murders."[135] He gives examples in his books concerning the evil effects of the suggestive nature of astrology. Thus astrological predictions or advice may cause people to do things they would otherwise never have done, and in some cases this has led to tragedy. For example, a woman murdered her son because an astrologer predicted he would lead a life of mental illness. The shattered mother went to jail, the astrologer went free.[136] The possibilities here are endless: A chart reveals a deformed baby, so an abortion results; a company may fail so the treasurer embezzles funds, etc.

We can only ask, how many crimes have been committed because of astrology?

3) *Economic loss*—With people asking astrologers for advice and counsel concerning financial investments and a variety of other economic decisions—such as gambling, weather prediction and crop yields, stock market fluctuations, etc.—there is plenty of room for financial loss or tragedy.

4) *Spiritual damage*—Since astrology is an occult practice (divination) condemned in the Bible, the worst damage an astrologer does is in helping to turn people away from God and Christ—to trust in a false religious philosophy. It not only prevents personal salvation, but opens the door to greater occult activity which may result in demonic involvement.

How does astrology lead people into the occult? A review of 14 "standard" astrological sources revealed three Sun-signs in particular that have occultic qualities—Pisces, Scorpio and Aries. Those born with these signs are supposed to be mystical, intuitive, psychic, spiritual, magical, clairvoyant, occultic, etc.[137] These persons are informed that they are *supposed* to be psychic or have psychic tendencies. Will not many of these people who are told of their "spiritual" nature try to fulfill their astrological or karmic "destiny" and thereby enter the occult?

5) *Psychological damage*—When clients make major decisions on the basis of astrological predictions or calculations—decisions relating to health, family and children, business, employment or future—then the door is open for potential tragedy. Such decisions are made upon an irrational and/or emotional basis only and not necessarily upon the basis of sound judgment or actual facts concerning the matter. Anyone claiming knowledge of the future is exercising an influence which can radically redirect a person's thinking. It may even lead some people into a decision-making process based on anxiety and the irrational. (When the element of demonic deception also enters the picture, one can be certain that harm will sooner or later result.)

"Astrological counseling" of sensitive people is fraught with potential dangers. What of those who are told they are born under Gemini, whose "influence" might result in split personalities? Will *some* Gemini who live under the burden of this knowledge be moved closer to the brink? What of those who try to live up to the "astrological nature" when it is really not in their nature? What difficulties or problems might this present?[138]

Even professional astrologers admit the dangers here. Astrologer-psychiatrist Bernard Rosenblum, an advocate of counseling by astrology, nevertheless warns, "...the bad reputation astrology must contend with is partly due to those astrologers who make definite predictions about people's death, divorce, or illness, and other statements that suggest the client must suffer the rest of his life with a difficult psychological problem in order to correct a karmic imbalance. Such astrologers are exhibiting arrogance and insensitivity in the extreme."[139]

Prominent astrologer Dane Rudhyar observes, "I have received many letters from people telling me how fearful or psychologically confused they have become after consulting even a well-known astrologer and being given a biased character analysis and/or predictions of illness, catastrophe, or even death."[140] Former astrologer Charles Strohmer admits, "Major sorrows came my way due to my involvement with astrology."[141]

Since most visits to astrologers concern issues that are of major importance to the client; for example, major decisions on money, health or illness, relationships, children, length of life or a spouse's life, etc., the opportunities for deception are endless.

6) *Moral damage*—Astrology has no moral character. First, almost all astrologers reject any absolute standard of morality and prefer a "situation ethics" approach where moral decisions are determined subjectively—largely by the whim and preference of the astrologer. Astrologer Alan Oken states, "No Path is the True Path, for in the Absolute there is no Truthfulness or Falsehood, no right and no wrong, no yes and no no."[142]

Second, many astrologers deliberately reject moral values. For example, astrologer John Manolesco observes, "Religious and moral values are declining, the fiction of free will, moral obligation, [and of] immutable, eternal values has been exposed for what it is—myth."[143]

Third, astrologers choose not to morally educate the public. Jeff Mayo, founder of the Mayo School of Astrology, emphasizes, "It must be understood that astrology: Does not moralize; the birth chart indicates weakness or strength in this respect: choice of action is the individual's."[144]

Finally, the astrologer is responsible to no one but his own beliefs, and the impersonal stars which have little or no concern over his behavior. For example, the kinds of tragedies seen above are easily justified on the part of the astrologer by an appeal to his client's "karmic destiny." Whatever his client's sins or tragedies in this life, they are only the results of conditions in a past life which have "predestined" them. For example, a number of astrologers serve the homosexual community. They may casually advise a client as to the time of his next affair, or explain to homosexuals that their sexual preference was "determined" by the stars.[145] Even one astrologer admits that "people used it [astrology] so often as an excuse, a justification for their weaknesses and shortcomings..."[146]

CONCLUSION: Two Real-Life Stories

The fact is that astrological predictions can have tragic results in people's lives. For many, the astrologer is "God" and his or her words have "divine" authority. Thus an astrological interpretation can, for many, be the equivalent of a personal revelation from God himself. Consider the following true stories that further compound the problem of astrological counseling. A young man consults an astrologer who informs him that the stars reveal he will marry young but that his first wife will not be the one "destined" for him.

Only his second wife will bring him "true happiness." The man deliberately marries young in order to get his first wife, that is to fulfill the prophecy, so that he will not miss finding his second wife who alone will make him happy. His first wife is a very good and devoted wife and bears him three children. But after the third child is born, the husband abandons his wife and family and later obtains a divorce on the grounds of his own complicity. He marries the second wife whom he believes is the one the stars have destined to make him happy. Yet within a few months she joins a cult and has made his life utterly miserable and he divorces her.[147]

Thus a single astrologer with a single prediction brings pain and tragedy into the lives of six people—three adults and three children. Now multiply this prediction power by millions of astrological predictions and advice given every year and you can see the potential for disaster. Far too many tragedies are "arranged" by astrological predictions. The pattern is clear: 1) clients are amazed by accurate self-disclosures; 2) these self-disclosures generate *trust*; 3) trust leads to deception; 4) deception produces unwise or immoral decisions and actions; 5) bad actions bring ruin or destruction.[148]

A second illustration reveals not only how easily astrology becomes a vehicle for tragedy but the reality of spiritual warfare hidden beneath the surface. Here we see how astrology produces an irrational fear and despair. It also paralyzes initiative and sound judgment, and can lead to suicide if not prevented. A certain woman was engaged to be married and felt that seeking the advice of an astrologer might be useful. After drawing the horoscope, the astrologer predicted the following: "Your engagement will break up. This man will not marry you. You will not marry at all, but remain single." The woman was devastated. She was so much in love with her fiancé she could not bear the thought of losing him. She became paralyzed with fear. She continually worried that the engagement would break up, that she would never marry. She finally resolved to put an end to her life, but on the day she intended to kill herself, a friend of her fiancé was able to stop her. Upon the advice of that friend she went for pastoral counseling, revealed her plight, repented and gave her life to Christ. Soon after that day, her fiancé also gave his life to Christ. Today they are married with several children and are quite happy. Nevertheless had it not been for Christ, the disaster which was set afoot by the astrologer would have happened.[149]

A Personal Word

If, as a Christian, you are now involved in some way with astrology, we would hope that the information in this book would cause you to stop your involvement.

There are two reasons why: First, as a Christian, your loving God warns you that astrology is one of Satan's philosophies, and we are not to seek for information from such sources. As we have seen in this book, evil spirits are the real power behind many astrologers. But second, the columns they write and books they author are also means to ensnare our minds and rob us of peace.

Ask the Lord to forgive you of your disobedience to Him and ask Him to supply all your needs. He will.

If you are wondering if you are a Christian, or you know that you never have placed your faith in Jesus Christ, we encourage you to receive Christ now. If you do want to receive Christ, just pray:

> Dear God, I ask Jesus Christ to enter my life and be my Lord and Savior. I recognize this is a decision that You take very seriously. I believe that on the cross Jesus Christ died for my sin and I receive Him into my life now. My commitment to You is that I will follow Him and not astrology. I ask for Your help in doing this. Amen.[150]

Notes

1. *The Los Angeles Times*, September 3, 1975, p. 1.
2. June Wakefield, *Cosmic Astrology: The Religion of the Stars* (Lakemont, GA: CSA Press, 1968), p. 22.
3. Charles E.O. Carter, *The Principles of Astrology* (Wheaton, IL: Theosophical Publishing House, 1977), p. 13.
4. Theodore Laurence, *The Foundation Book of Astrology* (Secaucus, NJ: University Books, 1973), p. 13.
5. Jeff Mayo, *Astrology* (London: Hodder, and Stoughton, 1978), p. 2.
6. Owen S. Rachleff, *Sky Diamonds: The New Astrology* (New York: Popular Library, 1976), p. 15.
7. For example, "Ascendant," "Aspect," "House," "Sextile," "Cusp," "Sesquiquadrate," "Imum Coeli," "Ecliptic," "Opposition," "Quadruplicity," "Quincunx," "Trine," "Zodiac," "Descending Node," etc.
7a. Neither is there agreement on the value of the aspects, which also leads to widely different interpretations.
8. John Anthony West and Jan Gerhard Toonder, *The Case For Astrology* (Baltimore, MD: Penguin Books, 1973), p. 1.
9. Lawrence E. Jerome, *Astrology Disproved* (Buffalo, NY: Prometheus Books, 1977), p. 1.
10. Bernard Gittelson, *Intangible Evidence* (New York: Simon and Schuster, 1987), p. 338.
11. The Gallup Poll for October 19, 1975. See R. B. Culver and P. A. Ianna, *The Gemini Syndrome: A Scientific Evaluation of Astrology* (St. Buffalo, NY: Prometheus Books, 1984), p. 2.
12. Derek and Julia Parker, *The Compleat Astrology* (New York: Bantam, 1978) p. 178.
13. "News and Comment," *The Skeptical Inquirer*, Vol. 9, no. 2, pp. 113-114. The May 1988 Gallup Poll indicated overall belief in astrology was down, but this poll did not include the aftereffects of the White House revelations.
14. Geoffrey Dean, "Does Astrology Need to Be True? Part One: A Look at the Real Thing," *The Skeptical Inquirer*, Vol. 11, no. 2, p. 167.
15. Derek and Julia Parker, op. cit., p. 60.
16. e.g., see Eden Gray, *A Complete Guide to the Tarot* (New York: Bantam, 1980), pp. 204-27; also Javane & Bunker's *Numerology and the Divine Triangle* (Para Research, 1980), which integrates numerology, Tarot and astrology as does John Sandbach's *Degree Analysis: Dwadashamsas and Deeper Meanings* (Seek It, 1983). Dane Rudhyar, Liz Greene, and Stephen Arroyo are three leading astrologers currently integrating psychology with astrology. See Joanne Sanders, "Connecting Therapy to the Heavens," *The Common Boundary*, January/February 1987, pp. 11-14; also Alice Howell, *Jungian Symbolism in Astrology* (Wheaton, IL: Quest, 1987). West and Toonder, op. cit., pp. 221-227; Roy A. Gallant, *Astrology: Sense or Nonsense* (Garden City, NY: Doubleday, 1974), pp. 14-19. Gittelson, op. cit., pp. 350-353; on medical astrology, see Harry F. Darling, M.D., *Essentials of Medical Astrology* (Tempe, AZ: AFA, 1981); Omar V. Garrison, *Medical Astrology: How the Stars Influence Your Health* (New York: Warner, 1973). c.f., Barb Bok and Lawrennce E. Jerome, *Objections to Astrology* (Buffalo, NY: Prometheus Books, 1975), p. 46; C. Norman Shealy, *Occult Medicine Can Save Your Life* (New York: Bantam, 1977), p. 117; Gallant, op. cit., pp. 115-116. On Hinduism and Theosophy, see James Braha, *Ancient Hinu Astrology for the Modern Western Astrologer* (N. Miami, FL: Hermetician Press, 1986); Edward K. Wilson, Jr., *The Astrology of Theosophy* (Tempe, AZ: AFA, 1982).
17. Dean, Part 1, op. cit., p. 167.
18. Joyce Wadler, "The President's Astrologers," *People Weekly*, May 23, 1988, p. 111; Gittelson, op. cit., pp. 352-353.
19. e.g., Mae Wilson-Ludlam taught the first accredited high school astrology course in 1972. The July, 1988 AFA Convention handbook and book tables indicated several astrologers taught astrology at high school or college campuses e.g., Louise Bronley at Emory University.
20. Culver and Ianna, op. cit., p. 2.
21. From M. Kurt Goedelman, "Seeking Guidance From the Stars of Heaven," *Personal Freedom Outreach*, July/September 1988, p. 5. This is probably exaggerated, although it is widely agreed that a significant number of major corporations do use astrology.
22. *The Los Angeles Times*, July 5, 1985, p. 1.
23. Henry Weingarten, *A Modern Introduction to Astrology* (New York: ASI Publishers, 1974), p. 28.

24. e.g., The American Federation of Astrologers in Tempe, Arizona offer tapes on this from past conventions. The July, 1988 convention in Las Vegas also offered courses on the subject.

25. *The Los Angeles Times*, July 5, 1985, p. 1.

26. Geoffrey Dean, "Does Astrology Need To be True, Part 2—The Answer is No," *The Skeptical Inquirer*, Vol. 11, no. 3, p. 262.

27. E. Howe, "Astrology," in Richard Cavendish (ed.), *Man, Myth and Magic: An Illustrated Encyclopedia of the Supernatural, Vol. 1* (New York: Marshal Cavendish Corporation), p. 149.

28. e.g., Culver and Ianna, op. cit., pp. IX-218. See Question 23 and our forthcoming text, *Astrology: Do the Heavens Rule Our Destiny?* (Harvest House, 1988).

29. John Weldon, *Hazards of Psychic Involvement*, unpublished, 1986, pp. 1-389. See the writings on the occult by Dr. Kurt Koch (e.g., *Between Christ and Satan* (Grand Rapids, MI: Kregel, 1962) and Dr. Merrill Unger (e.g., *Demons in the World Today*, (Wheaton, IL: Tyndale, 1972). Also see Edmond Gruss, *The Ouija Board: Doorway to the Occult* (Chicago: Moody, 1975), pp. 59-112; Merrill Unger, *The Haunting of Bishop Pike* (Wheaton, IL: Tyndale, 1971); Personal testimonies include Doreen Irvine, *Freed From Witchcraft* (Nashville: Thomas Nelson, 1973); Johanna Michaelsen, *The Beautiful Side of Evil* (Eugene, OR: Harvest House, 1982); Raphael Gasson, *The Challenging Counterfeit* (Plainfield, NJ: Logos, 1970); and Malachi Martin, *Hostage to the Devil: The Possession and Exorcism of Five Living Americans* (NY: Bantam, 1977).

30. See Merrill Unger, *Biblical Demonology* (Wheaton, IL: Scripture Press, 1971); C. Fred Dickason, *Angels: Elect and Evil* (Chicago, IL: Moody Press, 1975); and Merrill Unger, *Demons in the World Today*, op. cit.

31. Significantly, in eight of ten courses taken at random during the July 4-8, 1988 American Federation of Astrology convention in Las Vegas, NV, the astrology instructors admitted to having spirit-guides. The definition cited is from Merrill Unger, *Biblical Demonology*, op. cit., p. 119.

32. Apart from the literature that could be cited, this was admitted by most of the dozens of astrologers we talked with at the July, 1988 American Federation of Astrologers convention in Las Vegas, Nevada.

33. *The Los Angeles Times*, January 15, 1975.

34. Ibid.

35. Carter, op. cit., p. 14.

36. in Gittelson, op. cit., p. 350.

37. Clifford Wilson and John Weldon, *Psychic Forces* (Chattanooga, TN: Global, 1987), pp. 331-345.

37a. In addition, at the May 1988 AFA convention 20-year astrologer Rev. Irene Diamond told us the spirits personally led her into astrology and that all her books on astrology were produced by spirit dictation and/or automatic writing. The current AFA president, Doris Chase Doane, told us that the spirits' efforts through the occult Church of Light (founded by C. C. Zain) is "very important to the work of astrology."

38. Alice Bailey, *Esoteric Astrology* (London: Lucius Trust, 1982). This is volume 3 of *A Treatise on the Seven Rays*.

39. Margaret H. Gammon, *Astrology and the Edgar Cayce Readings* (Virginia Beach: A.R.E. Press, 1987) p. VIII.

40. Ibid., p. 15; reading no. 3744-3.

41. West and Toonder, op. cit., pp. 107-108.

42. Daniel Logan, *The Reluctant Prophet* (1980), pp. 63-65, 169-170.

43. Marcus Allen, *Astrology for the New Age: An Intuitive Approach* (Sebastopol, CA: CRCS Publications, 1979), pp. 2, 6. A brief perusal of over 500 books authored by astrologers at the July, 1988 convention. Many astrologers, if not most, were into other forms of the occult. This was also true for most of the astrolgoers we talked with.

44. "Sepharial," *A Manual of Occultism* (New York: Samuel Weiser, 1978), p. 3.

45. Sybil Leek, *My Life in Astrology* (Englewood Cliffs, NJ: Prentice Hall, 1972), p. 11.

46. Ibid., p. 12.

47. Ibid., pp. 19, 31, 48.

48. Doreen Valiente, *An ABC of Witchcraft Past and Present* (New York: St. Martin's Press, 1973), p. 21.

49. Ibid., p. 23.

50. Dean Rudhyar, *The Practice of Astrology* (New York: Penguin Books, 1975), p. 21.

51. Weingarten, *A Modern Introduction to Astrology*, op. cit., p. 77.

52. Richard Cavendish, *The Black Arts* (New York: G.P. Putnam's Sons, 1967), pp. 219, 222, 225.

53. Keith Thomas, *Religion and the Decline of Magic* (New York: Charles Scribner's Sons, 1971), chapter 21.

54. Ibid., p. 634.

55. Jerome, op. cit., p. 225.

56. Ibid., p. 76.

57. John Warwick Montgomery, *Principalities and Powers* (Minneapolis, MN: Bethany, 1976), p. 96.

58. Edward J. Moody, "Magical Therapy: An Anthropological Investigation of Contemporary Satanism," in Irving I. Zaretsky and Mark P. Leone, *Religious Movements in Contemporary America* (Princeton, NJ: Princeton University Press, 1974), pp. 362-363.

59. In 17 years of reading New Age, Eastern, psychic and occult literature this was acknowledged in every text read.

60. Gittelson, op. cit., pp. 348, 353.

61. Charles Strohmer, *What Your Horoscope Doesn't Tell You* (Wheaton, IL: Tyndale House, 1988), pp. 45-55.

62. Robert Leichtman, M.D., "Clairvoyant Diagnosis," in the *Journal of Holistic Health* (San Diego: Association for Holistic Health/Mandata Society, 1977), p. 40.

63. Derek and Julia Parker, op. cit., p. 129.

64. Jeanne Avery, *The Rising Sun: Your Astrological Mask* (Garden City, NY: Doubleday, 1982), p. 396.

65. Syndey Omar, *My World of Astrology* (Hollywood, CA: Wilshire Book Company, 1965), p. 21.

66. Ralph Metzner, *Maps of Consciousness* (New York: Collier, 1976), p. 126.

67. Parker, op. cit., pp. 88-96, 145.

68. Colin Wilson, *The Occult: A History* (New York: Vintage Books, 1973), p. 250.

69. Howe, in Cavendish (ed.), op cit., pp. 153-154.

70. Michael Shallis, "The Problem of Astrological Research," *Correlation*, Vol. 1, no. 2, pp. 41-46 from Kelly and Krutzen, "Humanistic Astrology: A Critique," *The Skeptical Inquirer*, Vol. 8, no. 1, p. 73.

71. Gittelson, op. cit., pp. 353-354.

72. Ibid., pp. 29, 306-308, 282-283.

73. Metzner, op. cit., p. 111.

74. Allen, op. cit., p. 6.

75. Rudhyar, *The Practice of Astrology*, op. cit., pp. 130, 136.

76. Leek, op. cit., pp. 19, 202.

77. Gittelson, op cit., pp. 348-349.

78. Isabel M. Hickey, *Astrology: A Cosmic Science* (Watertown, MA: privately published, 1974), pp. 275, 276.

79. Robert A. Morey, *Horoscopes and the Christian* (Minneapolis, MN: Bethany, 1981), p. 54.

80. Ronald Davison, *Synastry: Understanding Human Relations Through Astrology* (New York: ASI Publishers, 1978), p. 94.

81. Allen, op. cit., p. 117.

82. Rudhyar, *The Practice of Astrology*, op. cit., p. 8.

83. Davison, *Astrology*, (New York: ARC Books, 1970), p. 12.

84. Mayo, op. cit., p. 7.

85. Joseph F. Goodavage, *Astrology: The Space Age Science* (New York: Signet, 1967), p. XI.

86. For illustrations see James Sire, *Scripture Twisting* (Downers Grove, IL: InterVarsity, 1982).

87. James Bjornstad and Shildes Johnson, *Stars Signs and Salvation in the Age of Aquarius* (Minneapolis, MN: Bethany, 1971), pp. 36-90.

88. Gallant, op. cit., p. 111.

89. For a very brief review see Bjornstad and Johnson, op. cit., pp. 88-89.

90. In the thirteenth to sixteenth centuries astrology was variously practiced in the church, in part due to the influence of Thomas Aquinas.

91. Morey, op. cit., pp. 48-49.

92. Jeane Dixon, *Yesterday, Today and Forever: How Astrology Can Help You Find Your Place in God's Plan* (New York: Bantam, 1977), p. 6.

93. Ibid., pp. 7-9.

94. Ibid., p. 12.

95. Ibid., p. 502.

96. John Warwick Montgomery, *Principalities and Powers* (Minneapolis, MN: Bethany, 1976).

97. Letter on file dated June 2, 1986.

98. Clifford Wilson and John Weldon, *Psychic Forces* (Chattanooga, TN: Global, 1987), see section on Christian parapsychology.

99. Promotional brochure for AFA Golden Anniversary Convention included with product price list, Winter, 1987-1988. But a week-long visit to their July, 1988 convention revealed that many of the astrologers had spirit guides and practiced other forms of the occult. The President and First Vice President of the AFA are both spiritists.

99a. The Gauquelin research; Mark Urban-Lurain, *Astrology as Science: A Statistical Approach* (Tempe, AZ: American Federation of Astrologers, 1984), see pp. 1, 10-11, 32-33; Jeannette Glenn, *How To Prove Astrology* (Tempe, AZ: American Federation of Astrologers*, 1981), see p. 13.

100. Dean, Part 1, op. cit., p. 167. Urban-Luraine, op. cit., p. 1.

101. Dean, Part 1, op. cit., p. 175, citing I. W. Kelly, R. Culver and P. J. Loptson, 1986, "Arguments of the Astrologers: A Critical Examination" in Bisivas et al. (eds.), *Cosmic Perspectives* (Indias Science Circle, India).

102. Kelly and Saklofske, "Alternative Explanations in Science: The Extroversion-Introversion Astrological Effect," in *The Skeptical Inquirer*, Vol. 5, no. 4, p. 35. This contains a summary of the events.

103. Culver and Ianna, op. cit., p. 216. The controversy may be traced in *The Skeptical Inquirer*, Vol. 4, no. 2, pp. 19-64; Vol. 5, no. 4, pp. 62-65; Vol. 6, no. 2, p. 67; and Vol. 7, no. 3, pp. 77-82.

104. Michael Gauquelin, "Zodiac and Personality: An Empirical Study," *The Skeptical Inquirer*, Vol. 6, no. 3, p. 57.
105. Ibid., pp. 57-64.
106. Michael Gauquelin, *The Scientific Basis of Astrology: Myth or Reality* (New York: Stein and Day, 1973), p. 145.
107. Dean et al., "The Guardian Astrology Study: A Critique and Reanalysis," *The Skeptical Inquirer*, Vol. 9, no. 4, pp. 327-337.
108. Mechler et al., "Response to the National Enquirer Astrology Study," *The Skeptical Inquirer*, Vol. 5, no. 2, pp. 34-41.
109. Cited in Dean, Part 1, op. cit., p. 178.
110. Ibid., p. 173.
111. e.g., Gittelson, op. cit., p. 355.
112. Ralph Bastedo, "An Empirical Test of Popular Astrology," *The Skeptical Inquirer*, Vol. 3, no. 1, p. 34.
113. Kurtz and Fraknoi, "Tests of Astrology Do Not Support Its Claims," *The Skeptical Inquirer*, Vol. 9, no. 3, p. 211.
114. John McGervey, "A Statistical Test of Sun-sign Astrology," *The Zetetic*, Vol. 1, no. 2, p. 53.
115. Dean, Part 2, op. cit., p. 267.
116. Douglas Lackey, "Controlled Test of Perceived Horoscope Accuracy," *The Skeptical Inquirer*, Vol. 6, no. 1, p. 30; Dean, Part 1, op. cit., pp. 179-180.
117. Dean, Part 2, op. cit., p. 263.
118. Ibid.
119. Ibid, p. 267.
120. These are summarized in Kelly et al. "The Moon Was Full and Nothing Happened," *The Skeptical Inquirer*, Vol. 10, no. 2, p. 139.
121. Culver and Ianna, op. cit., pp. 169-179.
122. Kurtz and Fraknoi, op. cit., pp. 210-211.
123. Dean, Part 2, op. cit., p. 265.
124. Letters to the editor, "The Humanist," November/December, 1978, p. 24.
125. West and Toonder, op. cit., p. 155.
126. Weingarten, *The Study of Astrology*, op. cit., pp. 129-130.
127. Carter, op. cit., p. V.
128. S. Best, "Astrological Counseling and Psychotherapy: Critique and Recommendations," *Astrological Journal*, Vol. 25, no. 3, pp. 182-189 from Dean, Part 2, op. cit., p. 268.
129. Stephen Arroyo, *Astrology, Psychology and the Four Elements: An Energy Approach to Astrology and Its Use in the Counseling Arts* (Davis, CA: CRCS Publications, 1978), pp. 24-25.
130. Dean, Parts 2 & 3, op. cit.
131. Gittelson, op. cit., pp. 282-283.
132. Strohmer, op. cit., p. 51.
133. John Manolesco, *Scientific Astrology* (New York: Pinnacle Books, 1973), p. 125. c.f. Garrison, op. cit., pp. 147, 11-15, 137-146.
134. Manolesco, op. cit., p. 125.
135. Kurt Koch, *Satan's Devices* (Grand Rapids, MI: Kregel, 1978), p. 20.
136. Kurt Koch, *Between Christ and Satan* (Grand Rapids, MI: Kregel, 1962), pp. 11-12.
137. Bastedo, op. cit., p. 31. Frances Sakoian and Lewis Acker, *The Astrologers Handbook* (New York: Harper and Row, 1973), pp. 94-95.
138. Bok and Jerome, op. cit., p. 50.
139. Rosenblum, op. cit., pp. 120-121.
140. Book Review in *The Zetetic Scholar*, 1979, nos. 3 & 4, pp. 83-85, c.f. his *From Humanistic to Transpersonal Astrology* (Palo Alto, CA: The Seed Center, 1975), p. 12 and Manolesco, op. cit., p. 27.
141. Strohmer, op. cit., p. 55.
142. Oken, op. cit., p. 85.
143. Manolesco, op. cit., p. 33.
144. Mayo, op. cit., p. 4.
145. Jess Stern, *A Time For Astrology* (New York: Signet, 1972), pp. 210-215.
146. Allen, op. cit., p. 56.
147. Kurt Koch, *The Devil's Alphabet* (Grand Rapids, MI: Kregel, 1969), pp. 17-18.
148. Strohmer, op. cit., p. 47.
149. Kurt Koch, *Satan's Devices*, op. cit., pp. 20-21.
150. For growth in the Christian life, Francis Schaeffer's *True Spirituality* and J. I. Packer's *God's Words* are very helpful.